D1491179

Ed Young and Mac Richard

beauty
FULL

Becoming More

Than Just Pretty

CREALITY

All Scripture quotations, unless otherwise noted, are taken from
The Holy Bible, New International Version (North American Edition),
copyright © 1973, 1978, 1984 by the International Bible Society.
Used by permission of Zondervan Publishing House.

Any emphases or parenthetical comments within Scripture are the
authors' own.

Published in Dallas, Texas, by Creality Publishing.

Cover design and layout by Kirk DouPonce, DogEaredDesign.com
Cover photo by Ghislain & Marie David de Lossy, Getty Images

ISBN 978-1-934146-46-0

For our daughters,

LeeBeth, Landra, Laurie and Emily

Each of you has grown to reflect—
brilliantly and radiantly—the many facets of
God's beauty in all that you are. Strong and spirited,
wise and whimsical, or classic and compassionate,
you continually remind us of what God had in mind
when he hand-crafted woman and the true beauty
he hopes to reveal to the world.

Table of Contents

Acknowledgements

Without the selfless work, contribution and dedication of a team of people, a book like this would never materialize. I'd like to thank several of the people who helped make this book happen.

To Andy Boyd, Cliff McNeely, Katie Moon and Javetta Mercadel, thank you for your help in editing, researching and composing the words in the following pages.

To my family, thank you for putting God's true beauty into perspective each and every day.

And finally, to Mac. Thank you for your ministry, your example and most of all your friendship.

—Ed

So many people contributed time, talent, and insight to make this book a reality. To Ashley Austin and Teri Brown, thank you for your feedback, counsel, protection and editing throughout the writing of this book.

To Mom, thank you for introducing three hairy-legged boys to the beauty of unconditional love. To Julie, thank you for so freely sharing your beauty with me every chance you get. You have shown me the beauty of contentment, whatever our circumstances.

And, to Ed. I'll never be able to repay everything God has built into my life through you and Lisa. Thank you for your leadership, partnership, and friendship.

—Mac

In today's world of makeup and manicures, spa treatments and spray on tans, so many women are living in the shadows of true beauty. Rather than focusing on God's intent for soul deep beauty, we concentrate on the surface image in the mirror. Sadly, many of us look to the cultural definition of beauty as the standard measurement of our own self worth.

We hide behind the struggles of not being thin enough.
We beat ourselves up over not being fashionable enough.
We obsess over not being "pretty" enough.

But the skin deep beauty that society touts is a cheap counterfeit of the true beauty God has placed inside each and every one of us. In this book, our husbands teach us how to reclaim God's amazing gift and how we can reveal it in and through every aspect of our lives.

You may be wondering how two *men* can write a book that speaks to women about true beauty. After all, haven't men played a large part in distorting the definition of beauty into what it is today? But don't be so quick to discount their words.

The Bible is full of strong, passionate, real-life examples of what God has in mind when it comes to his design for beauty. And as lifelong students of God's Word, Ed and Mac have had the opportunity to research and communicate the truth about that beauty to thousands of women.

As husbands, they have continued to bring out our true beauty, even in the most difficult of times. On our worst days, they encourage us and remind us of the beauty God has instilled in our souls. And on our best days, they remind us of our beauty by showering us with compliments.

Finally, as fathers, Ed and Mac do all they can to underscore and highlight God's intended beauty in the hearts and lives of their daughters. And they strive to communicate to their daughters how truly beautiful they are in their fathers' eyes.

It is so easy to get caught up in the demands of society. But if we aren't careful, we can end up feeling inadequate and empty. This book will help you gain a clear understanding of beauty that will leave you feeling beauty *full*. And you will see how God's gift to you has the power to change not only your life, but also the lives of everyone you touch, forever.

—Lisa Young and Julie Richard

chapter one

SOMETHING

The room is completely sterile, even cold. The décor is a half-hearted attempt to hide its function, but instead screams, "This is a hospital room!" Here, in this room, a woman is welcoming her first child into the world. Her husband crouches by her head and holds her hand, nervous—OK, scared silly—trying in vain to "coach" her, to reassure her, to contribute in any meaningful way to the life-changing event they are both a part of. Sweat drips off their heads under the industrial-grade floodlights that illuminate the room. This setting will be the infant's first introduction to the world.

Forget Lamaze classes, *Discovery Channel* specials, or any other attempt to accurately convey the birth experience; nothing can fully prepare you for what happens in that room. And you can forget about the 'partition' that is a sheet strategically strung to shield the view. In the delivery room, there is nowhere to run and nowhere to hide. Unlike television, no amount of soft lighting or makeup can obscure the realities of birth.

And yet, in the midst of all this, there is *something* about the birth of a child. It is unique in that it is simultaneously soul-stirring and stomach-churning. You wouldn't trade it for anything in the world, but you certainly would not choose to experience it over breakfast.

Yet, when this child makes her dramatic entrance into the world, there is...*something*. *Something* in that moment draws us in at a soul depth. For once, the word miracle seems entirely appropriate. The arrival of a new life in this world calls *something* out of you, despite your inability to sufficiently describe or even comprehend it.

We all have those moments when we see or experience something that transcends mere physical senses; it literally penetrates our souls and draws us to itself. We can't explain it. And even if we could, we wouldn't want to diminish the experience by reducing it to words. But in those moments, there's *something* that attracts our very souls.

That *something* is the same thing God chose to illuminate in and through the heart of a woman. That *something*, and the reason it moves us at such a profound level, is the facet of God's character that he has stamped into the soul of every woman. That *something* is found in a woman's touch—

the touch with which God marked her soul; the touch with which she marks her world.

That *something* is beauty.

Inherent beauty

Proverbs 31:30 says, "…beauty is fleeting." The beauty referred to is physical attractiveness, prettiness. But beauty in its truest, most profound sense goes far beyond what our world settles for in its idea of attractiveness. It goes beyond good looks, perfect makeup or soft, flowing locks of hair. At its most elemental level, beauty is deeper. It's about being more than just pretty. True beauty is a reflection of a significant part of God's own character, his heart. And although beauty defies a concrete definition, we need to grow to understand what beauty is.

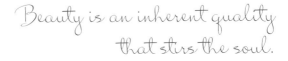

Beauty is an inherent quality that stirs the soul.

Underline that word *inherent*. If you don't have a pen, get one. Underline that word physically, underline it emotionally and underline it intellectually. Why? We want you to realize and see that authentic beauty is inherent. It is integral to the character and nature of God. And it is a part of who he has made you to be.

Everyone who has ever been born has been created in the image of God by God himself. This is true for men; it is also true for women. And part of his stamp on your life as a woman is this inherent beauty.

The fact that our culture values physical beauty so greatly and exalts it so highly points to the fact that beauty is an echo of God's eternal self. And because God has placed eternity in the heart of man (Ecc. 3:11), our desire for beauty only echoes that longing.

However, the fact that we so often settle and strive for mere physical beauty points to something else—our fallenness. Ever since the first bite of the forbidden fruit in the Garden of Eden, we have been fighting the temptation to sacrifice what is best and hard-won for what is easy and apparent. And we have settled for a counterfeit of beauty, a cheap imitation. To quench our longing for beauty, though, we must learn to see it for what it really is.

Beauty is every woman's gift. It is her gift from God, her gift to God, and his gift to the world through her. The gift of beauty is integral to a woman's soul; it's the *something* internal that draws you to her. A woman, as God fashioned her, cannot be understood, appreciated, or loved apart from beauty.

It is that part of her that longs to be longed for, to be

cherished. It explains, but also eclipses and transcends her desire to be physically attractive, to be pretty, no matter how powerful that desire may be or how suppressed and denied it may be. Any definition of beauty limited only to an external view diminishes and destroys the full power of this gift.

To understand the nature of this gift called beauty, think of an expensive painting or a tapestry. The more intricate a painting; the more finely woven a tapestry is, the more valuable it is.

Now, think of diamonds (Did we get your attention?). A diamond's value is determined by several things, one of which is the number of facets. Simply put, the more multifaceted a diamond is the more brilliant it is. The more brilliant a diamond is the more value it holds.

Now reflect back on the beauty of a woman. Little else in the world holds the brilliance of a woman. She is one of God's most intricate and multifaceted creations; she is one of his most valuable creations. Beauty is merely a reflection of that value.

Every little girl who is loved, nurtured, and valued longs to be considered beautiful. It is the wise parent, especially a father, who recognizes this need, builds on it, and establishes firmly in their daughter the belief in her own *inherent* beauty. And the loving parent directs the daughter to her heavenly Father as the essential Source and affirmation of that inherent beauty.

The psalmist writes,

"One thing I ask of the Lord, this is what I seek. That I may dwell in the house of the Lord all the days of my life to gaze upon the beauty of the Lord and to seek Him in His temple." —PSALM 27:4

Anything of beauty; any*one* of beauty is a reminder, a recasting of God's character and personality. This is why God issues this encouragement specifically to women in 1 Peter:

Your beauty should not come from outward adornment, such as braided hair and the wearing of gold jewelry and fine clothes. Instead, it should be that of your inner self, the unfading beauty of a gentle and quiet spirit, which is of great worth in God's sight.

—1 PETER 3:3-4

Contrary to traditional, legalistic teaching, this passage is not primarily concerned with hairstyles and hemlines. This is first and foremost an encouragement, a calling to women to cultivate the authentic, genuine beauty they were created to carry and communicate—beauty that transcends, precedes, and therefore nourishes physical appearance. Read that passage again. It begins by declaring, *"Your beauty…"*

The fact of every woman's inherent beauty is assumed! In the heart and mind of God, your beauty is a given. Only in the hearts and minds of people, maybe even in your own mind, is your beauty in any doubt.

Only when you look to people—a man, children, your father, other women, yourself—rather than the Lord for the affirmation of your beauty do you reap doubt, loss of esteem, anxiety, and seeds of insecurity.

Consider Jesus

Consider Jesus, God in the flesh. The Bible tells us very clearly that Jesus was not physically attractive.

He grew up before him like a tender shoot,
and like a root out of dry ground.
He had no beauty or majesty to attract us to him,
nothing in his appearance that we should desire him.
—Isaiah 53:2

It's likely that Jesus never would have made the cover of *GQ.* Yet, we repeatedly see in him that *something* that drew people, that caused others to want to hang out with him, to be around him, to just breathe the same air that he breathed. There it is again: that *something* that is beauty.

Nowhere in the life of Christ, or anywhere else in Scripture for that matter, does beauty manifest itself as weakness. Any portrayal of beauty as empty or vapid is a cheap counterfeit of genuine beauty. The gift of beauty is always intentionally engaging and voluntarily vulnerable, never feeble or frail. Godly beauty carries a very real strength and vigor that lovingly challenges and irresistibly invites. It is the very thing that unexplainably draws others in. And people aren't drawn to something that is weak or frail.

This is the authentic character of beauty—this *something* illuminated in the soul of a woman—that we (women *and* men) have to personally accept, adore and admire, because we live in a world that has significantly distorted and diminished it. We ache, spend, work, travel, and all too often settle for a cheap imitation or fabrication of beauty. But in order to fully understand what God intended when he created women, we have to truly appreciate genuine, soul-deep beauty.

It has to be illuminated as the gift in the soul of a woman through which God blessed Creation. It is the gift God designs every woman to carry and personify in her every relational transaction. Can you imagine a world in which God had never declared, "It is not good for the man to be alone" (Gen. 2:18)? It's scary to even consider.

It is the gift God gave to all of Creation. It is the gift he gave to Adam in Eve. It is the gift a mother gives to her daughter. It is the gift a man is to affirm and defend in the life of every woman in his life. It is a gift to be enjoyed, appreciated, protected, cultivated, celebrated, and illuminated by everyone.

The illumination of this gift produces true women's liberation; it releases you and strengthens you to be the woman God created you to be; independent of the world's expectations; independent of the lies people have spoken into your life; and independent of your own doubts and insecurities. Recognizing the power of this gift liberates you to celebrate your femininity, to discover and reveal your beauty to the world, and to feed the fire of those relationships that nurture and value it.

As with every blessing and freedom he gives, God has also given you a significant responsibility. We live in a world that is desperately parched for even a small taste of beauty. Your responsibility is to reveal it to the world around you. God has given this gift to you and he is waiting for you to give it to others in a way that reflects his personality, his love, and his purposes.

The Bible records this lyric in the book of Psalms:

"I sought the Lord, and He answered me. He delivered me from all my fears. Those who look to Him are radiant. Their faces are never covered with shame."

—Psalm 34:4-5

Read that last line again. "*Their faces are never covered with shame.*" Because so many women don't understand the fact that they are beautiful; because they've fallen prey to the world's view of beauty, they cover themselves. This may not manifest itself literally, for many women unsuccessfully try to reveal their beauty by revealing their bodies. But that, too, is a way of covering. It's covering their true identity, their true gift, their true beauty—beauty that goes beyond just being pretty.

But a woman who looks to God for her validation, whose relationships provide her consistent affirmation, and who understands her inherent value to God, is radiant. Her life radiates the life of God, the love of God, the very beauty of God. And she reveals that beauty to the world around her.

Illuminated

Take a moment and think about a woman you know who possess a gentle and quiet spirit; a woman who is full of joy and peace. Think of a woman who laughs easily and is content with her life. Do you have one in mind?

This woman may not necessarily be pretty. Odds are good that she won't appear on the cover of *Cosmo* or glide down a runway in Paris in a couture gown. But we can guarantee you one thing without even knowing her name or seeing her picture: she is undeniably, unashamedly, and stunningly beautiful. No doubt about it. Every single time.

Can you think of anyone who wouldn't want to know that woman? Is there a life that is not blessed and improved for having known and loved her? Is there any man anywhere worth his salt who doesn't want to fan the flame of that gift of beauty in his bride, his daughter, his girlfriend or his mother? Is there any woman who doesn't want to *be* that woman?

Remember 1 Peter 3:3-4: That kind of beauty doesn't fade. It doesn't drop with gravity and years. It doesn't go away. It is God's gift to women, to every woman. And he has purposefully and intentionally placed it in you.

This book is about *how* to recover and reveal this gift through your life, from the inside out.

chapter two

IMAGE RESOLUTION

You know this image. You've seen the picture a thousand times. It's possible that you've studied it or even gazed at it in person. But because the image is so distorted, you'd never know that it portrays one of the most well-known faces in the entire world.

Now, look at this image.

This is the same picture as the first one. It's just been refined so you can clearly see all the subtle details, colors and features. And now you can tell what it is.

The difference between these two images is solely a function of *image resolution*. The colors, the perspective, and the composition are all the same; but they are distorted in the first one and in just the right combination in the second one.

When it comes to men and women—the role we are each to play and the image we are each to portray—the world has distorted God's intended image. We've skewed the colors, the perspectives and the composition. But in Genesis 1:27, God gives us his perfect design for complete image resolution:

So God created man in His own image. In the image of God, He created him, male and female, He created them.

This verse offers a message more practical and profound than many other passages of Scripture. It tells us that God stamped into the heart of man parts of his persona that he did not primarily stamp into the heart of a woman. And, conversely, he stamped parts of his personality into the heart of woman that he did not give primarily to man.

This stage of creation stands as the only time God examined his work and said, "This is not good." But he wasn't talking about his creation itself; he was talking about the condition of his creation.

When God saw man by himself he said essentially, "It is not good that man is alone. Man should not be left alone to portray my image and character and nature, because there is more to me than he can show by himself. Man needs help doing that."

To sufficiently bear the image of God, man needed help. Specifically, he needed a "suitable helper." And so God created woman.

Beauty lost

When it comes to reflecting the image of God, men and women must work together and come to understand their roles. Men primarily reflect the image of strength. Women primarily reflect beauty. Obviously, in bearing the image of

God, there is some overlap between men and women: there is strength in a woman's inherent beauty and there is even beauty in a man's inherent strength.

But sin distorts the image of God. Sin takes what God has designed and twists and contorts it to the point that it is no longer recognizable.

> In sin, a man distorts the image of God in silence or in violence.

The silent, passive, disengaged man betrays the strength God has entrusted to him. He distorts the image God intended.

Go back to the Garden. Satan approaches Eve. She engages. She struggles. She falls. But where is Adam? He's silent. He doesn't even whisper, "Uhh, do you think we really ought to do that? I don't know. No, don't take that." He does nothing. His impotence indicts him.

Swing the pendulum the other direction and God's image is distorted in the overly aggressive, violent man. Whether physically, emotionally or verbally abusive, a violent man distorts, betrays and abuses the strength God has placed within him; he distorts it. Both extremes are rooted in sin; both extremes warp the image of God.

Women, too, can distort the image of God by misusing and misunderstanding this gift called beauty. Remember, we're not talking about the superficial façade; we aren't talking about just being pretty. We're talking about that innate, inherent quality; that *something* that draws people in, that magnetizes them.

> In sin, a woman distorts the image
> of God by hiding or striving.

Any woman who is hiding her beauty from the world is distorting the image of God. But as we mentioned earlier, hiding doesn't necessarily mean physically covering your body.

Many women attempt to hide their true feelings from those who are close to them. These women use sarcasm and spite to put up a wall, hiding the emotional beauty that God has placed in their lives. Other women attempt to hide their own insecurities by gossiping or back-biting. But no matter how much we try to justify it, that too is hiding your beauty from the world.

Part of a woman's innate beauty is the fact that God has created you as an emotional, vulnerable and caring being. And that beauty is something to be enjoyed, something to be revealed and expressed.

By the same token, there are women who appear outwardly beautiful, but in actuality they're striving to maintain an image—but it's the wrong image. They're white-knuckling the steering wheel of their lives in an attempt to maintain full control of everything around them. That was Eve's sin in the Garden.

Eve's sin was not biting into the fruit. Eve's sin was attempting to wrestle control from God. She no longer trusted God to provide for all of her needs, wants and desires. Instead, she decided to control her own destiny. And she did her best to rip the control out of God's hands.

This is the battlefield for a woman's soul: the battle to control everything about her. And the attempt to control life completely may manifest itself in a myriad of forms:

- Striving to control her appearance and overcome nature.
- Striving to control her children's behavior and their appearance.
- Striving to control her husband and his behavior.
- Striving to control her relationships in general.
- Spinning plates of career, family, and personal pursuits to create the illusion of "having it all" and having it all together.

Regardless of the symptoms, it is the dis-ease of striving, the grasping for control that, at its root, is not beautiful. It is not inviting. If anything, it is a stone fortress that repels.

This is Eve's legacy, her estate passed down since the injection of sin into this world.

But whether it's an abusive man or a woman who strives to maintain total control, a distorted image of God's reflection in the human heart is the result of one factor: fear.

> Fear is the primary
> enemy of beauty.

Granted, there are several other factors that spawn off of fear, but fear is the primary source of a distorted image. Whenever beauty is obscured, fear has won. It is fear that drives a woman to hiding from the world or striving to maintain control of circumstances beyond her grasp.

In those moments when you feel your beauty threatened or jeopardized, you now know why. So how do you get your beauty back? How do you begin to clear the image of beauty God has placed in your life?

Beauty recovered

Remember 1 Peter 3:3-4? Your beauty is assumed by God. It's inherent in you. But there's a part of that verse that points to the recovery of the beauty that is lost in hiding or striving. God's creative genius is manifested in the beauty of a woman through the *"unfading beauty of a gentle and quiet spirit, which is of great worth in God's sight"* (1 Peter 3:4).

We in the Richard household had a spiritual crisis over this very verse about 10 years ago. We're like the Loud Family on the old *Saturday Night Live* skit. We are loud people. Our kids are loud. Our dogs are loud. If we had a fish, it would be loud. We are a loud family. And when my wife Julie was in a Bible study that covered this verse, she came home almost in tears saying, "Gentle and quiet spirit?! I don't have a gentle and quiet bone in my body. How can I be beautiful if I'm loud?" (For the record, she was not asking these questions in soft, hushed tones.)!

Julie's an extrovert by any measure you want to use. But she absolutely possesses a gentle and quiet spirit. This passage of Scripture is talking about that quality of a woman's spirit, of her soul, that is gentle and quiet because she is content, because she is at peace, because she is not hiding her beauty; she isn't striving for total control, white-knuckling her world. She is content and at peace with who God has made her to be and the role she plays.

A gentle and quiet spirit is rooted in contentment and peace.

You may be an extrovert; you may be the life-of-the-party personality type. Or you may be an introvert; you may be a woman who really and truly recharges by being completely alone. But that doesn't necessarily mean you have a gentle and quiet spirit. A gentle and quiet spirit isn't something that is determined by the volume of your voice, the number of friends you have or the fact that you spend more time alone. A gentle and quiet spirit is more about your position before God and the way you portray the beauty he has inherently given you.

The world we live in day-in and day-out is marred by wars, scarred by wounds, and damaged by silence and violence. It's a world in desperate need of more beauty, of *your* beauty.

Women, you have a privilege that men will never know. It is the privilege of revealing your beauty and sharing it with the rest of the world. But to do so, you must understand what it takes to cultivate, protect, and ultimately, reveal that beauty.

Cultivate Your Beauty Diligently

Beauty, though innate, does not just appear. You have to cultivate that beauty, that quiet and gentle spirit. And it begins with rest.

Rest. Make time for yourself to renew your heart, to heal and recharge your spirit. True rest begins in your relationship with God. It is your responsibility to set aside the time to pursue God, to get to know him through prayer and reading his Word.

This is time where you're not answering the phone, you're not changing a diaper, you're not running carpool, answering email or anything else. It's just you and God. Remember, we're talking about the God who has given you the gift of beauty. God is the one who says your beauty is inherent, that you possess a beauty that touches eternity. What better use of your time can you imagine than knowing, loving and growing in your relationship with him?

There's an amazing passage in the Song of Solomon that speaks directly to this cultivating of beauty.

> *Do not stare at me because I am dark,*
> *because I am darkened by the sun.*
> *My mother's sons were angry with me*
> *and made me take care of the vineyards;*
> *my own vineyard I have neglected.*
>
> —Song of Solomon 1:6

The bride is speaking to her bridegroom. She's saying, "No, no, don't look at me. I have cared for the vineyards of everyone around me—everyone's except my own."

Most women have trouble caring for their own vineyard, cultivating their own beauty, because they are so focused on caring for others. And this is important. But to truly cultivate your beauty, you must learn to also take time just for yourself. And do not apologize for it. It's something that you need; something that enables your beauty to shine.

The biblical term for this type of rest is *Sabbath*, which means literally "to cease and desist." Sabbath equals rest. And the Bible says the Sabbath was made for people (Mark 2:27). It is God's intention that we get rest to recover regularly. So cultivate your beauty by resting your soul.

Protect Your Beauty Fiercely

Just as beauty has to be cultivated, it also has to be protected, fiercely. Proverbs 4 says,

> *Above all else, guard your heart, for it is the wellspring of life.* —Proverbs 4:23

"*Above all else.*" Does that leave any question as to the priority that God places on this assignment? In the Jewish mindset, the heart is the wellspring of life; it is the birthplace of every motive, thought, word, and action; it is where beauty resides.

But this idea of protecting your beauty tooth and nail is not restricted to the Old Testament mindset. Look at the words of Jesus:

"Do not give dogs what is sacred; do not throw your pearls to pigs. If you do, they may trample them under their feet, and then turn and tear you to pieces."

—MATTHEW 7:6

You have to value your beauty. You have to know and believe that it matters to God, and therefore it should matter to you and anyone else around you. Protect your beauty.

The primary line of defense for your beauty comes down to one word: relationships. Because God created woman as a relational being, her relationships play the primary role in protecting the gift of her beauty. Her friendships, romances, and ultimately her marriage will either protect and deepen her beauty or they will rob and devalue it. So protect your beauty by first surrounding yourself with those people who are willing to also protect it.

Reveal Your Beauty Faithfully

Cultivate your beauty diligently. Protect your beauty fiercely. And, finally, reveal your beauty faithfully. This is where you show the world what God has placed in you and what others have helped you protect. This is where you show the world the beauty that has always been present but may not have been prominent. This is where you express your beauty in God-reflecting ways by living out the truth of Psalm 34:

I sought the Lord. I went after God, I pursued Him, and He answered me. He delivered me from all my fears. Those who look to Him are radiant. Their faces are never covered with shame. PSALM 34:4-5

The promise of God concerning beauty is this: when you pursue him, when he is your focus and your Portion, you will radiate his personality, grace, love, acceptance, security, power and truth.

A woman who looks to God for her value and who understands what she means to him, to others and to herself, receives the promise that her life will radiate the life of God, the love of God, the beauty of God. And it is in that life that a woman accurately and beautifully bears the image of God—in full resolution for all the world to see.

chapter three

DIAMONDS

In its rough, uncut form, a diamond appears to be nothing more than an ordinary rock. When it's first unearthed, it bears little resemblance to the crystalline gem that eventually captures and reframes light with such breathtaking clarity. To the untrained eye, this hunk of earth appears to be no more valuable than any other piece of dirt. It is only after a painstaking process of excavation, polishing, and cutting that its value is fully realized; only then does the once coal dust-covered crystal become something beautiful and brilliant and desired.

While natural beauty is inherent within each stone, the long process of refinement is what allows light to reflect and refract more brilliantly and shine more brightly. It's the process of cutting facets into a diamond that adds value to the diamond. And as we saw briefly in chapter one, the more facets a diamond has, the more valuable and beautiful it becomes.

God has shaped a woman's heart with multiple facets. Little else shines as brightly or reflects as much radiance. But as we have also seen, that beauty must be protected if it is to be fully reveled and appreciated. The safer a woman is in her relationship with God and with other people, the more her brilliance and beauty will shine through and in her life. But this brilliance and beauty is not dependent on merely *feeling* safe. She has to actually *be* safe, because that is when the facets of a woman's heart will shine clearly for everyone to see.

There are four facets in particular that distinguish the feminine character from the masculine character. Unfortunately, these facets are often downplayed and discounted in a misguided attempt to achieve equality with men. And while equality in the workplace, at school, in the voting booth and in the community is beneficial to society, the quest for equality has often caused both men and women to negate and discard the very facets that make women unique and beautiful. And it is these four facets that God has chosen to focus and reflect through the prism of a woman's heart.

Facet #1: Nurture

Every woman is created with a unique ability and innate need to nurture. But, again, this is not something that is random or unexpected. Look at how God describes himself:

"Can a mother forget the baby at her breast and have no compassion on the child she has borne. Though she may forget, (God says) I will not forget you." —ISAIAH 49:5

That is the kind of God we serve. We serve a nurturing God. And when he wanted to reflect this eternal, immutable facet of his personality, he used the heart of a woman, of a mother, to put it in temporal terms we could understand. Women have the God-given ability to see the personal, emotional needs of those around them much more clearly than men. And this gift is something that God wants every woman to use in order to glorify him and reflect his beauty through her.

But as he does with every other God-given, God-honoring gift, Satan vigorously attacks this facet of a woman's heart. And he does this by convincing women to look first to other people to fill their relational needs rather than looking first to God. But whenever a woman seeks through human relationships what only God can provide, this nurturing facet becomes distorted and clouded.

Florence Nightingale Syndrome

The potential for nurturing run amok manifests itself in what we call the Florence Nightingale Syndrome. Florence Nightingale was a nurse in England during the late 19th-century. Her entire life was devoted to nursing others, particularly British soldiers fighting in the Crimean War.

As a vocation, nursing is a noble pursuit. As a relationship model, nursing creates incredibly unhealthy and damaging patterns. A woman who loses herself completely in "helping" others while neglecting her own faith, self, and perhaps even her family obscures the divine stamp of nurturing that God wants her to display. And ironically, the Florence Nightingale Syndrome ultimately becomes less about others and all about her—*her* helping, *her* being there, *her* just-the-right words, *her* how-does-she-do-it-all persona that just amazes everyone around *her*.

This facet can also be distorted in the overprotective, overbearing concern for a child or spouse. It moves from a caring issue into a control issue. This is the striving side of nurturing—striving to change those around you. In a single woman, it will usually result in her latching on to an inordinately needy man who is attracted to her "helpful" nurturing. He feeds her need to be needed and, in turn, she robs him of the opportunity to become an authentic, God-honoring, leading man.

If you see this tendency or drift toward Florence Nightingale, you think—many times subconsciously—*"He's such a good person deep down inside, I can help him bring it out…I can change him."*

Allow us to put on our pastor hats and lovingly encourage you with this simple truth: You can't change him.

The ditches of divorce are littered with broken-hearted women who thought that if they could just get him down the wedding runner, *then* they could change their man. First of all, it's not your job to change anyone. The only effective, eternal agent of change in a person's life is Jesus Christ.

Second, you don't have the ability to change a person. Dr. Jonathan Cude, a gifted and accomplished Christian marriage and relationship therapist in the Dallas/Fort Worth area, explains it like this:

> You cannot hope to change a person's thoughts or actions by unscrewing the top of his head, depositing the thoughts you want to be there (or, even, *ought* to be there), screwing his head-top back on and having that person behave according to the thoughts that you placed in his mind.

If it sounds like we're being a little harsh on this point, it's only because we have seen it played out too many times. And we want to help you avoid the disastrous outcomes from these behaviors.

If any of what we just talked about does apply to you, God says, "I can redirect you. I can help you polish off the facets of your life and learn to reflect the beauty that I've given you."

The first way that he redirects you is by reminding you that he is the lone source of your nurturing power; he is the one who nurtures you. You plug into that power by daily spending time with God. Don't simply look inward. Instead, learn to look upward and ask, "How is my vertical relationship with God?" Take time to read his love letter to you, the Bible, and make sure you spend time praying to and talking with him. Because when you allow God to nurture the foundation of your life, your relationships will reflect his love. And that's when his beauty will truly begin to shine through you.

Facet #2: Security

The second facet of a woman's beauty is that of *security.* Try this exercise. Take ten seconds and imagine a place of real beauty. Just close your eyes and allow your mind to drift there.

. . .

No matter what picture of beauty you painted in your mind's eye, it is most likely truly vulnerable. A pristine mountain panorama, a newborn child, a delicate flower, or any other beautiful thing is vulnerable to a number of disastrous possibilities—whether it's through a natural or man-made disaster.

Like any of these beautiful scenarios, a woman's beauty is also vulnerable. It isn't weak or passive, but it is regularly threatened. This is why a woman has to know in her soul that she is safe for her beauty to shine through. But that source of security, like the nurturing facet, must come first from the source of true security—God.

God is a God of security. It is a part of who he is. Part of that security is found in truth, not lies. That is why Christ described himself as Truth (*John 14:6*). Lie to a man and he'll get mad, but probably move on (and likely forget it, given a few days or weeks). Lie to a woman, and it will not be forgotten or glossed over. In lying to a woman, you have told her that she's not safe or secure in that relationship. And without that truth, without that security, her true beauty will not shine through.

> *And you also were included in Christ when you heard the word of truth. Having believed, you were marked in him with a seal, the promised Holy Spirit,…*
> —EPHESIANS 1:13-14

God is the God of security. And, in Christ, we are secure.

When a woman turns to anyone else first for this security,

she is asking that person for the impossible, the improbable; for that which only God can provide.

God promises to take care of our security daily. He cares and provides for you down to the clothes you wear and the food you eat.

> *"Therefore I tell you, do not worry about your life, what you will eat or drink; or about your body, what you will wear. Who of you by worrying can add a single hour to his life? So do not worry, saying, 'What shall we eat?' or 'What shall we drink?' or 'What shall we wear?' for the pagans run after these things and your heavenly Father knows that you need them. But seek first his kingdom and his righteousness and all these things will be given to you as well."* —MATTHEW 6:31-33

When you anchor your security—personally, daily, and eternally—to God's truth, you are liberated to trust people and to understand how truly safe you already are.

Facet #3: Intuition

One dictionary definition of intuition is: an extra sense for situations, discernment, keenness in perceiving and understanding. Can anyone intelligently argue that women don't excel in this arena more than men? Of course not, because this is another facet of a woman's heart. It is yet another facet of the divine that reveals the brilliance of God's handiwork in a woman's life.

Women's Intuition

The Holy Spirit gives women a unique insight into areas that need to be avoided. When a woman has a bad feeling or sensitivity to a certain situation that she or her family is getting ready to enter, she can say, "Wait a minute. That's not a place I need to be." Or, "That's not something we need to do." There may not be a clear, compelling reason, but it is often through a woman's intuition that God will communicate about possible dangers in life.

The Bible says that God is omniscient, all-knowing. He knows the number of hairs on our head as well as the anxious thoughts in our minds. It's something that can't be explained or understood. And God has supernaturally blessed women with an insight into some of this unexplainable knowledge through the person of the Holy Spirit. We like to call it "woman's intuition."

With God's Spirit, his wisdom, and insight, this facet of intuition is an amazing tool in the heart and hands of a woman. But in a woman's life, the upside of intuition should be balanced with a fair amount of caution.

The challenge lies in remembering that while God's intuition is infallible, no human being's is. Many times, a woman's intuition can be significantly clouded by her feelings and emotions. And feelings are not always accurate.

Proverbs speaks directly to this:

Who can say, "I have kept my heart pure; I am clean and without sin"? —PROVERBS 20:9

You have to always allow for the possibility that your feelings are not reflective of God's perspective.

This is not to suggest that feelings and emotions are liabilities. Far from it, for God has feelings too. The Bible says that our sin grieves the heart of God and that God rejoices when a sinner repents. So feelings and emotions are not all bad. It's just that ours are not above reproach or beyond muddled motives.

Jesus said in Matthew 10:16, "Be as shrewd as snakes and as innocent as doves."

We need to be very cautious and smart as we deal with feelings and emotions. Feelings can be fickle and freaky and they can go up and down.

Too many times, we have heard people say about a marriage situation or a job situation, "I'm not happy. And God just wants me to be happy. So, I am going to leave this relationship or this job or this town or this church. I'm going to find somebody or something that makes me happy 24/7."

That is *never* the nudging of the Holy Spirit. God never promises us happiness. He promises us joy.

You may be thinking, I like this idea of joy, but I'm not sure I understand what it is. What exactly is the difference between happiness and joy? Well, you're asking the right question.

Joy can be defined as the positive confidence I possess by knowing and trusting God regardless of the circumstances.

Joy is inner delight derived from an intimate relationship with Christ. Happiness is circumstantial, but joy is relational. No matter what life brings my way, no matter what the circumstances, if I have this inner delight derived from an intimate relationship with Christ, joy will flood my soul. It's the peace that surpasses all understanding.

–Excerpt from *Outrageous, Contagious Joy*
by Ed Young (Penguin 2007).

Oftentimes, it takes intuition to be able to tell the difference between a nudging by the Holy Spirit and a gut feeling that may actually be the result of some bad sushi. Don't live life solely based on feelings. Instead, turn to God and allow him to cut the facet of intuition into your beautiful heart.

Facet #4: Community

The fourth facet of a woman's heart that distinguishes her is *community*. Women are inherently, intuitively, and intentionally more relational than men. They desire and fuel community. Interestingly, there is no community without *communication*. Some studies show that women speak an average of 14,000 more words per day than men.

Women have this stamp of community in their lives because it again reflects the heart of God. He is the God of community. The entire Bible is God's record of his desire and drive for community.

In Genesis, even before God created man and woman, he was in perfect community with himself: God the Father, God the Son, and God the Holy Spirit. The miracle and mystery of the Trinity frames God as Triune—One in three and three in One. He is relational within himself.

Then, he created humanity. Why? For relationship. For community. Not because he needed it, but because he desired it. He placed Adam and Eve in the Garden of Eden, a place created specifically for community.

Once sin entered the world, God didn't negate his desire for community with man. Instead, he provided another avenue to community through the Old Testament sacrificial system. The sacrificial system facilitated community between the divine nature of God and the fallen nature of man. And it ultimately foreshadowed the perfect sacrifice for community, his son, Jesus Christ. The cross of Christ is the ultimate offer for community: If we would accept him and invite him into our hearts, we can have true community with God.

We see community once again in the book of Revelation, in the most soul-filling relational moment the world will ever know: When God has established that new heaven and new earth, the Bible says that he *dwells* there with everyone who has been redeemed by Christ. The Bible tells us in the last chapters of Revelation that the glory of God is among his followers there in that place. And God communicated his desire for community with us in nearly every page of his word to us.

There is no community without communication.

Have you ever compared the messages that women leave on voicemail compared to the messages that men leave? Think about it. Guys leave a message like this: "Hey, this is Bill. Call me. Later."

A woman's voicemail message is more like this, "Hi, this is Jill, and I was just driving down the street, and thought about you. Hope you're doing well. I was having this feeling and I really wanted to talk to you. I'm not sure where you are. Did you fly out to L.A. today? I don't know." Then a cut-off sound.

The next message is, "Oh, I'm sorry. I got cut off…so, where was I?…"

God endowed women with this great capacity for community and communication. And as yet another expression of his love, he offers ample direction for reflecting this gift throughout the Bible. Look at Proverbs 25:

A word aptly spoken is like apples of gold in settings of silver. —PROVERBS 25:11

Do not let any unwholesome talk come out of your mouth, but only what is helpful for building others up according to their needs, that it may benefit those who listen. —EPHESIANS 4:29

May the words of my mouth and the meditation of my heart be pleasing in your sight, O Lord, my Rock and my Redeemer. —PSALM 19:14

So we see throughout Scripture the fact that God wants community with us—from the beginning until the end and beyond. That just shows how he desires that community with you and me. And this drive in the heart of God is stamped in the heart of a woman. You are wired for relationships. Because in your relationships is where your beauty will shine brighter than ever.

These four facets of a woman's soul—nurture, security, intuition, and community—comprise incredible power and undeniable beauty. They hold the power to reflect the light of God's personality and character into every life, situation, and moment where they are fully realized. But outside of healthy community with and consistent guidance from God, they can also distort and blur not only the beauty of a woman, but also the very image of God.

The gift of this inherent beauty and brilliance calls for a response: You have a responsibility to cut and polish these facets in your own life so that the world—your world, your relationships, your environment—sees a true image of God's light in and through you.

chapter four

WHAT BIG LIES YOU HAVE

Very early in our marriage, my wife Julie and I (Mac) decided that we would help each other do what we could to take care of ourselves physically. We promised each other that would do our best to eat well, exercise, get the right amount of sleep and generally try to care for the bodies God had given us. We weren't talking about getting narcissistic about our physical health; we were just going to do our best to take care of ourselves.

And it was with that conversation in mind, just a few days later, that I was responsible for picking up dessert for an at-home date night we were going to have. On my way home I stopped by the grocery store and, with our mutually agreed-upon decision, thought, "Julie wants me to help her stay healthy. I'll buy a healthy dessert!"

Trying to be a supportive husband, I passed by the bakery and the gourmet dessert selections. I ignored the ice cream freezer. The whole time I was thinking, "Surely no woman ever had such a sensitive husband this early into her marriage!"

And as an expression of my love and devotion for Julie, I picked up a box of Snackwells® cookies and proudly took them home.

After dinner, Julie opened the grocery bag, took the cookies out, looked at me, and then said, "Huh, Snackwells."

But it wasn't until days later when we were in the middle of a very sincere marital "conversation" that Julie explained to me that I had really wounded her by buying Snackwells cookies.

When she told me this, I said, "Babe, you're going to have explain that to me. I thought it was just cookies. I don't understand what the issue is. I was just trying to be supportive of our mutual decision. I'm sorry."

Choking back tears, she told me, "When you bought those cookies I thought it was your way of telling me I was fat."

"What?! First of all, you're nowhere close to fat. Second of all, you are giving me way too much credit for putting way too much thought into a dessert!"

But I began to understand something right then and there. And it's something that isn't just true about Julie.

Whether they are in high school, middle school, middle

aged and married or single and young, this is a subject that preys upon the hearts and the minds of all women in general.

The root of lies

One recent survey showed that women stress and anguish over their body image or their physical appearance throughout any given day almost as frequently as men think about sex. That's a sobering statistic. And it means that though beauty isn't reserved for the physical looks, appearance plays a huge role in whether a woman feels beautiful.

Appearance does matter. But not for the reasons that our sex-crazed culture thinks. Satan has crafted some beautiful lies targeted directly at the hearts and minds of women. They include:

- Your worth is determined by your weight.
- Magazine cover-thin is the ideal.
- Cosmetic surgery is your only ticket to peace.
- Your figure is your greatest asset or your greatest liability.
- If you've got it, flaunt it.

Every single one of these statements and all the variations of them grossly disfigure and destroy the truth about what

God says about your body and your appearance. And every one of these lies is rooted directly in the fall that occurred in the Garden of Eden.

It's easy to blame our culture for these lies. But here's the deal: the world is doing exactly what the world has always been doing: fueling and feeding on your fears through the lies Satan communicates to you. This is nothing new.

In Genesis 2, God gave Adam some ground rules (chronologically, Eve had not been created yet):

> *The Lord commanded the man, "You are free to eat from any tree from the garden, but you must not eat from the tree of the knowledge of good and evil, for when you eat of it, you will surely die."*—GENESIS 2:16

A Simple Conversation

Now for a lot of people, Satan is a mythological character. They think of a little red man running around with horns and a pitchfork and a forked tail. He shows up, sits on your shoulder and seductively tells you to do bad things. Opposite to this little cartoon character, of course, is his angelic counterpart who tries to get you to do good things.

But when we turn Satan into a cartoon, something to merely laugh at, we underestimate the power and ability our worst enemy has to derail our lives. Satan is not mythological. He is real. The Bible tells us that he is like a lion, prowling about, looking for those he can destroy. And Satan is at the root of the Tree of the Knowledge of Good and Evil. But to fully grasp how Satan operates, we need to first understand more about who he is. And the Bible gives us the ability to do this.

> *The serpent was more crafty than any of the wild animals the Lord God had made.* —GENESIS 3:1

But not only is Satan evil, he's also extremely effective. Look how he worked Eve over.

> *"Did God really say you must not eat from any tree in the garden?"* —GENESIS 3:2

He didn't just show up in the garden with horns and a pitchfork and command her, "Eve, rebel against God; rupture the relationship for all those who will come after you. Don't believe God. You can determine your own fate. Put yourself on the throne of your life."

That's not how it happened. Instead, he just started a simple conversation with her. He just planted that little seed of doubt in her mind and in her heart.

Here's a question: Why did Satan go after Eve? Man had

already been created. Adam was there for the taking. So why Eve? The answer to this question lies within who Satan really is, his biographical sketch.

First of all, Satan was originally one of God's angels. He was an angel named Lucifer, and he was an angel of light. We read this in the book of Ezekiel in the Old Testament.

The second thing that we know about Satan is that he was originally beautiful. When he was living in his fullest glory as an angel of God; he was a stunning creature. He was pleasing to the eye. He captivated souls. The problem is that the primary soul he captivated was his own. He was completely consumed with himself.

And because he thought so highly of himself, Satan envied God's beauty and God's authority. So, he orchestrated a heavenly revolt, a coup d'etat. And God, who would not relinquish the throne, who bows to no one else, cast Lucifer out of heaven forever.

Now, think of how hateful Satan must have grown. Not only did he not overthrow God, but he was cast out of the very place he wanted to rule. And ever since his expulsion, everything that Satan does is in direct opposition to everything that God does. He is ultimately acting out of jealousy and envy.

Third, Satan is the root of death. Jesus says in John 8 that he is a murderer from the beginning, and the father of lies. Any dishonesty, any deception that you and I encounter or that comes out of our lives, ultimately traces its root back to Satan.

Now when you understand all that, you begin to understand why Satan went after Eve. Remember, God created woman with his own inherent beauty in her heart. And because or that, Satan envies the beauty of every woman.

Here's something else to think about. Where does life come from? Yes, it comes from God in concert with man. But it is women who are the vessels for life. Women give birth. And because each woman carries those components of God's character—beauty and life—she is immediately despised and envied, and therefore targeted, by Satan.

The fruit of lies

Now that we understand the roots of that tree, we can better understand the fruit that it yields in Satan's heart and mind. The first thing that is produced is hatred. And that is particularly powerful towards women.

Hatred

That's right; Satan hates women. He's not a big fan of men, either, because we too are created in the image of God. But he holds woman in special contempt. Anytime you see violence done to a woman—physically, emotionally, spiritually, or in any other way, shape or form—just know that Satan is at the root of it. That doesn't negate the responsibility of the person doing the damage, but just know that the root is Satan's hatred of women.

This hatred isn't reserved for others, though. It includes the hatred that a woman assumes for herself as well. When you don't give yourself credit, when you can't receive a compliment, when you downplay the good that you have inside of you, it's traceable back to the poisonous tree of Satan's hatred.

Obsession or Neglect

The second fruit produced in Satan is that of either obsession or neglect. And when women partake of this fruit, as far as their bodies are concerned, they have the tendency to drift into one of two camps. The first camp would be a woman obsessing over her body image, always anguishing and worrying about it. In extreme cases, this obsession can spiral into eating disorders of varying degrees of severity.

Or, the pendulum swings to the other extreme, and a woman completely neglects her body. She believes Satan's lies and resigns herself to thinking, "My physical appearance doesn't really matter. It's just selfish, shallow, and superficial to put too much concerted effort into caring for my body or appearance. So instead of taking care of my physical life, I'm only going to focus on my spiritual life."

But in either case, those women are believing two lies

straight from the pit of hell. Neither obsession nor neglect honors the God who created you. Who you are is a gift from God. And that gift, including the physical aspect, is to be treasured, guarded, and cherished; not neglected.

We have to get past this false dichotomy that we place between the physical and the spiritual. In God's economy, the physical *is* spiritual. It's all the same. In fact, in the book of Romans, God obliterated any imagined line between the two:

> *Therefore, I urge you, brothers, in view of God's mercy, to offer your bodies as living sacrifices, holy and pleasing to God—this is your spiritual act of worship.*
> —ROMANS 12:2

How you care for your body is a direct reflection of how much you appreciate God's creative genius and handiwork in your life. When you choose to eat right, get sufficient rest, and work out regularly, you are communicating volumes to God about how you feel about him. And that's exactly what he wants. It's your spiritual act of worship!

Isolation

And then the final piece of fruit that Satan produces; the final lie that women can fall prey to, is the lie of isolation. When you believe all these other "beautiful" lies, you will wind up feeling completely alone. And as a result, you begin to build walls around your life that ultimately cause you to feel even more alone. When you don't allow someone in to compliment you, to encourage you, then you are falling prey to Satan's attack and you contribute to your very own isolation. When you don't recognize the creative genius of God in you personally, spiritually *and* physically, you contribute to the isolation, to that sense of alone-ness.

This is what Satan ultimately wants. He wants to distract you from the love of those around you. He wants you to think that it's just you against the world. He wants you to believe that your beauty is something that needs to be hidden and that the only way to protect it is to downplay or neglect all that God has created in your life. And when you believe those lies from Satan, then he wins.

Don't allow yourself to be fooled. The lies are real. And they are devastating in both their effect and their reach. To one degree or another, they lay claim to the heart of every woman, particularly in our lust-saturated culture. But for all their reality, devastation, and boldness, they cannot withstand the truths of God. They wither in the fiery light of his glory and truth about what it means for you to be truly beautiful. And defeating these lies, recapturing the ground surrendered to them, requires roll-up-your-sleeves hard work. And actually, it requires a Body of Work.

chapter five

A BODY
OF WORK

Appearance matters, but not the way many of us think. Culture says that appearance matters because that is where your worth is; that's where your value is kept. But that's not why it matters. Appearance matters because of what it communicates about your connection to and understanding of God's image.

How a woman carries herself, how she dresses and presents herself in front of others conveys an important message to those people who see her. When they look at here, they are looking at the very image of God. That image can either be portrayed accurately or inaccurately, depending on what she reveals.

Before we get any further, though, it's critical that we remember our understanding of what authentic beauty truly is:

Beauty is an inherent quality that stirs the soul.

Given the fact that beauty is a spiritual thing; given the fact that the heart and character of God is imprinted in anything and anyone who is beautiful, when we talk about body image, it ultimately comes down to a heart issue. Body image is not merely a product of body fat percentage, stature, structure, hair color, hair texture or anything. It is a spiritual and emotional issue first and foremost; one that has physical manifestations.

Battle for beauty

In the last chapter we discussed the lies Satan whispers to you. And if you find yourself in any way bound or shackled by the lies of Satan concerning your body or appearance, remember what Jesus says. To overcome the lies and see the truth, you've got to understand that this is much more than a physical issue. It is first and foremost a spiritual issue.

"Our struggle is not against flesh and blood but against the rulers, against the authorities, against the powers of this dark world, and against the spiritual forces of evil in the heavenly realm." —EPHESIANS 6:12

This is spiritual warfare. And it is a battle that Jesus Christ has already won on the cross. But you have to own that battle. Sadly, though, many women don't understand the fact that the battle is over. And they are continuing to fight an enemy that has already been defeated. Don't fall victim to the loser. Instead, submit to the victor, Jesus Christ. And then appropriate that victory in order for it to matter where you live day in and day out.

There is a danger in acknowledging Satan, in giving him too much attention. The result is that we forfeit too much power to him. You're better served to focus on that which is authentic, that which is true, and good, and life-giving. And this is where we turn our attention to the Tree of Life and the fruit it can produce in your life.

The first piece of fruit from that tree is the *fruit of enjoyment*. Rather than hatred, you should enjoy your body, your physical appearance. Your physical self is something to be enjoyed and cared for because God gave it to you. And his gifts are good and perfect.

Your physical self is something to be enjoyed and cared for because God gave it to you. And his gifts are good and perfect.

There's a passage of Scripture that you need to memorize, cling to, and quote to yourself on a regular basis if you are going to reap the benefits of this fruit.

I praise you because I am fearfully and wonderfully made. Your works are wonderful. I know that full well.
—PSALM 139:14

And this, then, is how you should pray about this subject:

God, thank you. Thank you for my straight/curly hair. Thank you for my body. Thank you for my nose and ears. Thank you. Today, I am going to enjoy it, because, God, you made me. Today, Lord, I am going to care for it because you gave it to me.

The second piece of fruit from the Tree of Life is the *balance of truth*. If the lie that you are being told is the lie of either obsession or neglect, then in God you can find the balance of truth between contentment and stewardship: Turn to God and learn to be content with who you are, with who God created you to be, and become committed to caring for what he has given you. The way this should play out in your daily life is: do the best with what God has given you.

In God there is a balance of truth between contentment and stewardship.

We have a spiritual responsibility before God to care for our physical bodies. And God addresses this responsibility through Paul's letter to the Corinthians:

> *Flee from sexual immorality. All other sins a man commits are outside his body, but he who sins sexually sins against his own body. Do you not know that your body is a temple of the Holy Spirit who is in you, whom you have received from God. You are not your own. You were bought at a price. Therefore, honor God with your body.* —1 CORINTHIANS 6:18-20

"You were bought at a price." The price paid for you—body and soul—was Christ's death on the cross. But understand the correlation that he's making. This is a point and a counterpoint. He says, "You (your soul and your body) were bought a price. And now you need to recognize the opportunity and the responsibility that you have to care for that body that was paid for."

And within all of that is the concept of contentment. In that is an incredible peace that says, "You know what? I love God, and therefore I'm going to find and live in that balance between being content and caring for what God's given me."

And naturally, this entire topic speaks directly to how women should dress. But at this point, many women may put up a wall of defense and assume that pastors are anti-fashion. But we're not saying that you need to wear a burlap sack everyday and never dress fashionably. But you've got to consider where fashion and faith meet.

Remember: Appearance matters because of what it communicates about your relationship with God. And the first rule of communication is, consider your audience. You have to think about what other people are thinking about when you're communicating with them. Are you giving too much away?

Part of the allure of beauty is mystery. There's mystery in the heart of God. There's mystery in the heart of a woman. And there should be mystery to a woman's body as well, unless she's dealing with her husband. In the context of marriage, the mystery is to be revealed and shared. Where a woman's body is concerned, in marriage, enjoy one another by revealing all the details of that mystery. But apart from the marriage relationship; outside of those intimate marital moments, communicate the mystery of God as you communicate the beauty of God. Leave something to be desired about the mystery.

One final piece of fruit that is produced by the Tree of Life is intimacy. In the place of the isolation that comes from believing Satan's lies, the Tree of Life yields the fruit of intimacy. Truth and life always lead to intimacy, toward genuine connectedness with God and with other people.

One day, as Jesus was teaching, the legalistic scholars of the day threw a woman at his feet that had been caught in the act of adultery. They threw this woman at the feet of Jesus and said, accusingly, "What we do with someone like this? You talk about forgiving sins; you talk about the fact that you can absolve people of their wrongdoings before God, but the Law of Moses says she is to be stoned. What would you have us do with her?"

This is a volatile situation. They were trying to trap Jesus and get him to condemn her and deny her a connection with him. But the Bible says that Jesus just knelt down and wrote something in the sand. He didn't answer his critics immediately. But this wasn't because he didn't have an answer. In fact, his answer was genius. He looked up and said, "Go ahead and stone her. But, the first rock is to be thrown by the one of you who has no sin in his life."

He didn't abandon the Law of Moses, nor did he condone what she had done. It was the perfect answer. Can you imagine the Pharisees' frustration? They could do nothing but slowly walk away. Now that's a dramatic moment. But it pales in comparison to what came next.

At this point, it was just Jesus and this woman. Jesus straightened up and asked her, "Woman, where are they? Has no one condemned you?" "No one, sir," she said. "Then neither do I condemn you. Go now and leave your life of sin."

Jesus saved her life physically, yes. But he also saved her life spiritually and emotionally. Jesus doesn't condemn you. He loves you as you are. And he expects you to love him back with what he's given you. Because that's how you find true intimacy with him.

The 110-pound gorilla

Have you ever heard someone say this when a subject remains apparent but unaddressed: "There's an 800-pound gorilla in the middle of the room"?

In context of A Body of Work, it might be more appropriate for us to address the 110-pound gorilla in the middle of the room: What about elective surgery? This is, after all,

Nip/Tuck nation and home of *Dr. 90210* and countless other makeover shows.

Here's the easy answer: There's not a verse in Scripture that says "Thou shalt not go under the knife for purely cosmetic reasons." Nor is there a verse that condones or endorses it. And where Scripture is silent, we are left to resolve questions personally and prayerfully with godly counsel.

Here's the essay answer: Like everything else dealing with your appearance, it's a heart issue. If you are single, it is between you and God. If you are married, it is between you and God and your husband. If you are a student, there are significant medical and emotional reasons to delay even considering such a life-altering, body-altering decision. If you find yourself more often than not wrestling with the lies we covered in the previous chapter, you are not at a point where you are ready to consider cosmetic surgery. You are still determining whether you are going to live out of God's truth or Satan's lies.

Cosmetic surgery cannot fill a spiritual or emotional need in your heart that God has gone to such great lengths to satisfy. Using cosmetic surgery to satisfy those needs is like using a band-aid to treat compound fracture; it isn't appropriate, nor is it sufficient.

An enhanced figure—by itself—has never captured the heart of man worth capturing. It has never saved a marriage that wasn't already doomed. None of these is reason enough to risk general anesthesia, surgery, and recovery.

Understanding those caveats, in the event that you are currently walking closely with God, you are intimately connected with him and you have struck that balance between contentment and caring for your body, pray about it. At that point, if you feel the liberty in Christ and understand the risks inherent in any surgery; if you see it as a gift to be enjoyed by you (and by your husband if you're married), then proceed with caution and freedom.

Remember, how you carry yourself, how you dress and how you present yourself in front of others conveys an important message. Appearance is more than just appearance. It's a communication about your connection. So make sure you are communicating the right connection to your heavenly Father.

Chapter 6

THE S-WORD

Throughout our ministries, we have had the privilege of performing hundreds of weddings, each of which was preceded by premarital counseling. And, with some degree of regularity, we've had prospective brides sit in our offices and communicate something like this:

> "We are so excited to be getting married and can't wait to do this premarital counseling. But, before we begin, we do need to establish one important ground rule. Make sure that nowhere in the ceremony does the word submit rear its ugly head, okay? Good. Now let's begin."

We understand where that comes from. We understand the pushback to this controversial word, because it usually carries with it a negative spin on the idea of dominion and control. In our current marriage climate, *submission* is the real S-word when it comes to how husbands and wives relate to one another.

When we think the S-word, we think doormat. We think roll over, taken advantage of. To us living in the 21st century, it does feel a little Neanderthal. Surely we have progressed past this antiquated, calcified view of a woman's role in marriage. Haven't we?

For the record, we share in the repulsion to that notion of marital disequilibrium. It is repugnant and stifling, and it is a stench in the nose of God. But our pushback to submission betrays a gross misunderstanding of the biblical command.

It is, after all, still there in the Bible. Two thousand years, burned bras, and cracks in the glass ceiling have not managed to erase that oh-so troublesome verse in Ephesians:

Wives, submit to your husbands as to the Lord.
—EPHESIANS 5:22

Say the word out loud: *Submit.* Are you still alive? You didn't pass away from just saying the word. It's not an ugly word. It's not a life-ending word, but a life-giving word as we'll see throughout the next two chapters. What we'll discover together is that there are five essential facts that make submission everything God intends it to be.

Submission is not limited to women.

First, we need to understand that biblical submission is not limited to women. (We can hear the *Amen*s and *Hallelujah*s from here!) It's not. Yes, the Bible does say, "Wives, submit to your husbands," in Ephesians 5:22. But what has been largely omitted (primarily by male teachers, pastors, etc.) for centuries is the verse that immediately precedes it:

> *Submit to one another out of reverence for Christ.*
> —EPHESIANS 5:21

In God's economy, relationship works *because* people submit to each other, no matter the relationship, whatever it may be. Lest we think the verse in Ephesians is a typo, God reiterates the very same idea in Philippians (among other places throughout the New Testament):

> *Do nothing out of selfish ambition or vain conceit, but in humility consider others better than yourselves.*
> —PHILIPPIANS 2:3

Whatever relationship you're in, it will work better if both parties submit to each other.

Submission is the intentional prioritization of another's needs, wants, and desires above our own.

Where marriage is concerned, we are very concerned. Divorce continues its cancerous attack on God's gift of marriage and family. Even more disturbing is the fact that the stats don't particularly improve when you move from the general population to the church.

The root of every single divorce is a familiar relational enemy: Selfishness. It's an oldie but a goodie. Straight-up selfishness causes spouses to begin keeping score, measuring affection, and determining "winners" and "losers" as if there could even be a winner in such a warped paradigm of marriage. If husbands and wives would root out selfishness, divorce would not just plummet, it would evaporate. Relationship works well and best when both parties submit to each other. Selfishness is the root of relational rot. And, rarely is selfishness unilateral.

When marital conversations are punctuated with expressions like,

You always…
You never…

Her husband never…
I remember when we first got married…

"selfish ambition and vain conceit" are having their way. Submission is the intentional prioritization of another's needs, wants, and desires above our own. When both people in a relationship submit, both of their needs, wants, and desires are satisfied. No score-keeping, no record of wrongs suffered, and no worry about whether or not my needs are being met.

Submission is not person-centered.

Second, biblical submission is not person-centered. A lot of people get hung up on submission because they erroneously think they're really submitting to another person for the sake of that person. But that is not the case.

Yes, we submit to one another but look at how strategically God included the motivation for our submission: "…out of reverence for Christ." When you submit to another person, in biblical submission, you are doing it as an expression of worship. You're submitting to that person out of your relationship with God.

This is where the submission issue breaks down for so

many people, men and women alike. For women in particular, though, if you submit for your husband's sake only, then it really is *Sub-mission: Impossible.* But if it is an outgrowth of your love affair with Christ and your gratitude for his submission to the Father's will on your behalf, then you start to fuel submission with the power of the Holy Spirit.

This challenge is what God describes in Genesis when he seeks out Adam and Eve after they had broken trust with him. Immediately after Adam and Eve fell, the Bible says that God was looking for them. Specifically, God walked into the garden in the cool of the evening and called out to Adam and Eve. Here's how the Bible captures this moment:

> *Then the man and his wife heard the sound of the LORD God as he was walking in the garden in the cool of the day, and they hid from the LORD God among the trees of the garden. But the LORD God called to the man, "Where are you?" He answered, "I heard you in the garden, and I was afraid because I was naked; so I hid."*
> —Genesis 3:8-10

Hiding from God. This same God who loved them, who created them, who provided everything they would ever need. They were hiding from God.

And then when He called them out, they confessed their

sin to Him. And God began to explain to Adam and Eve what they had done, the consequences of their sin. Look at what God said to Eve specifically in Genesis 3:16. To the woman, he said, "I will greatly increase your pains in child-bearing. With pain you will give birth to children. *Your desire will be for your husband and he will rule over you* (emphasis added)."

This may be one of the most misunderstood passages in the entire Bible. God is not issuing a *prescription* in the wake of the fall; he's not saying how he is reshaping the heart and desires of the woman. Instead, he is issuing a *description* of her new reality in the wake of the fall. He's telling her what her life will be like because she has sinned. Because sin has now entered the world, this is woman's reality.

The word *desire*, in the original Hebrew, means *a turning*. And what God is describing here is that Eve has turned her attention, turned her desire from God to a person. Her desire now is no longer for God to validate her, no longer for God to justify her existence and to give her fulfillment and meaning. From this point forward she will battle her desire and the consequences of her desire for a man to satisfy those yearnings in her.

Do we need to detail just how inadequate any man is to fully validate or fulfill the soul longings of a woman? Every time a woman looks to a man for that, she is setting herself up for deep disappointment. On the best day of his life, at his absolute alpha male peak of performance, a man simply cannot validate a woman's existence. Only in God does that happen.

And so God is saying, "Eve, understand this is the result now. And because you in your sinful nature have turned away from me, in his sinful nature he will try to rule over you. In sin, a man will try to lord that over a woman. A man will try to dominate a woman."

Isn't it fascinating that, in marriage, men are commanded to serve and women to submit. For the health of the relationship, for the good of both parties, husband and wife are called to tasks that run counter to their sin nature.

That's not an accident.

In the paradigm of marriage (or any other relationship for that matter), our relational rivers are flowing, pure, and consistent. God calls men to serve and women to submit with the full knowledge that we will have to rely on his grace to make it work. In full dependence on him for that grace and that power, a fully yielded woman becomes more fully who God created her to be *because* she is bearing the image of her Creator.

He is the image of the invisible God, the firstborn over all creation. For by him all things were created: things in heaven and on earth, visible and invisible, whether thrones or powers or rulers or authorities; all things were created by him and for him. He is before all things, and in him all things hold together. —COLOSSIANS 1:15-17

Submission in God's economy embodies the image of Christ's unconditional, active, dynamic love. It is a privilege to submit in this type of relationship.

Umbrella fella

I (Ed) hate to carry umbrellas. I generally consider them a nuisance, but Lisa, on the other hand, always carries an umbrella if there's a chance of rain. Awhile back it was raining cats and dogs—I mean, it was coming down in sheets—and Lisa was prepared.

She said, "Honey, get under the umbrella with me so you won't get wet."

As she held the umbrella in her hand, I attempted to walk side by side with her underneath its protection. The problem was that I am taller than Lisa and ended up walking hunched over with half of my body exposed to the pelting rain. She tried to compensate by moving the umbrella over but that didn't work either. Needless to say, we were both getting drenched.

She said, "This is not working."

"No, it's not." I agreed.

So she handed me the umbrella. I took the umbrella in my hand, she snuggled in close to me and we walked in concert together through the rain without getting wet. We even got in a couple of kisses along the way. It was a beautiful thing.

That simple story illustrates both a husband's and a wife's job description in Scripture. For men: service. And for women: submission. The umbrella represents the spiritual authority within marriage. Men are called to be umbrella fellas, to be servant leaders in marriage as a representation of Christ in that covenant relationship.

God's call to submission is often misrepresented as a chauvinistic, paternalistic relic of repressive, male-dominated cultures. What this view overlooks is the fact that a wife's submission *follows* her husband's service. If the man is holding up his end of the marital covenant, he initiates sacrificial love and unselfish service. He establishes the priority of his wife's needs above his own as his primary desire in the marriage.

He does this in imitation, and only in the power, of Christ.

Husbands, love your wives, just as Christ loved the church and gave himself up for her to make her holy, cleansing her by the washing with water through the word, and to present her to himself as a radiant church, without stain or wrinkle or any other blemish, but holy and blameless. —EPHESIANS 5:25-27

So, the woman who submits to this kind of man is actually submitting to her own best interests! It establishes order. It provides protection. This kind of servant leadership and godly submission is a beautiful thing. Again, look at the creative genius of God! Look at how brilliantly he set this up, wired us up, and continually lifts us up through this gift of marriage.

Unfortunately, this ideal raises significant questions in the heart of many women:

What if I'm not married to the ideal man, or anything close to the ideal man?
Does the submission model implode?
Am I off the submission hook?

What these women are really asking boils down to this: *How do I make the "ideal" reality when I don't live in an "ideal" world, much less with an "ideal" man?* They're wondering if they can (ought to?) move from a mindset of *Mission: Impossible* to *Sub-Mission: Possible.* It's a good question…

chapter seven

SUB-MISSION: POSSIBLE

When I (Mac) was teaching this in our church, in the days leading up to the message, Julie and I talked a great deal about this subject. I have learned over the years to trust her intuition and insight, particularly when I'm dealing with a live-grenade issue like submission in marriage. At one point in this conversation, she said to me, "You know, I realized that I really don't have much of a problem with submission. And then I realized it's mostly because we agree on so much. The only time I really have trouble with submission is when we disagree."

There was a pregnant pause while her last sentence hung in the air for a second, and then she looked at me and said, "This IS hard!" There is no such thing as submission until there is a disagreement. Agreement is not submission. Submitting means trusting and letting go. And God gave this imperative in marriage because he knew that there would be conflict.

He knew that there would be differing opinions. And he knew that at some point a decision would have to be made. And so when the decision has to be made, the husband hopefully and prayerfully has earned the credibility and the trust and the respect for the wife to submit and allow him to make that decision. She has to choose to trust him and to trust that in the event he is wrong, God is bigger than his mistake. So, ultimately, she will submit because of her relationship with Christ.

In a godly relationship—particularly in marriage—you don't submit for the sake of the other person, or to be defined or validated by that other person. You submit out of reverence for Christ. It is for him and through him that a godly wife submits to her husband.

But there are so many factors conspiring against every woman seeking to mimic Christ's example in submission. For one, part of the American myth is self-determination. We're all about "life, liberty, and the pursuit of happiness." It says so right there in the Declaration of Independence. The only problem is that God never promises happiness. Happiness ebbs and flows with happenings. He promises joy and peace, which he unleashes in response to our obedience, and which we offer in response to his love (Ed has written an entire book on this subject entitled, *Outrageous, Contagious Joy*—check it out!).

Also, submission just simply flies in the face of our innate sin nature. Ever since Eden, we have wrestled with our desire to chart our own course and determine our own destiny—to say nothing of the consequences of those desires.

There is, however, one external factor that more than any other significantly influences a woman's desire to submit: *her father*.

It just is what it is. More often than not, Dad is the first source of validation in a woman's life. A girl appropriates the degree to which she is inherently beautiful, treasured, and cherished proportionately to the degree her father communicates those truths to her. As such, for better or worse, fathers wield incredible power in shaping their daughters' perception and experience of God.

We are both fathers of daughters. And we have to be very intentional about giving them a positive picture of their heavenly Father. What does that mean in practical terms? It means spending quantity and quality time with our girls. It means planning one-on-one dates with them…and not breaking them. It means keeping our promises to them. It means listening to them—really listening! Do you hear us screaming? Girls need to talk things out and, dads, we need to learn how to listen. It means communicating to them that Dad will protect them: they are safe and secure in our care. It means showing them with our attitudes and actions, day in and day out, that they are unconditionally loved no matter what.

Dads are frequently healthy, God-honoring, although imperfect, vessels for God's love in the hearts of their daughters. If a woman is not taught and instructed how to find her validation and worth in a personal, loving relationship with God, she will then look to other men for that validation. And, as we've already established, no man is capable of carrying the validation load for you. He wasn't designed to bear that kind of weight.

But the woman who seeks her validation in God understands that a man can enhance and liberate who she is rather than define who she is. From fathers to boyfriends and boyfriends to husbands, the wheel turns. And recognizing this cycle often turns the key that unlocks the door to submission in the heart of a woman who has resisted or refused to submit in her marriage.

With this dynamic in mind, the submission question still remains for a woman in marriage: *How do I make the "ideal" reality when I don't live in an "ideal" world, much less with an "ideal" man?* Remember the working definition of *submission:*

Submission is the intentional prioritization of another's needs, wants, and desires above our own.

It is intentional, it is thoughtful, it is selfless, it is God-like. And it is tough. But God has provided a foundation of facts to support submission. These facts are like pillars anchored in his personality and character, and they sustain the winds of cultural changes, personal choices, and spiritual challenges.

Submission in marriage means, **submit**.

The first foundational fact of submission is this: The biblical concept of submission in marriage does mean *submit*. There is no linguistic loophole that gives us another more palatable, less challenging meaning. As we pointed out in the last chapter, the New Testament is essentially a case study in submission. The Son of God submitted to the Father's will for our sake, leading to our submitting to Christ in response to his sacrificial death, burial, and resurrection. And, as an outgrowth of our submission to him, we willingly submit to each other for his sake:

> *Do nothing out of selfish ambition or vain conceit, but in humility consider others better than yourselves.*
> —PHILIPPIANS 2:3

Submission rests on respect.

Second, submission rests on respect. Turning back to God's essay on marriage, Ephesians 5, we see this:

> *The husband is the head of the wife as Christ is the head of the church. His body of which He is the savior. Now as the church submits to Christ so also wives should submit to their husbands in everything.*
>
> — EPHESIANS 5:23

Respect begins with an appreciation for the role of a husband. He is called to model Christ. Take it from two men who frequently miss the mark, it is a daunting task. Even if the man in that role in your life is less than you want him to be, or less than God has called him to be, you will generate more respect for him when you appreciate the gravity of his role.

Respect rests on sacrificial initiative.

The third pillar of submission flows out of the second one: Respect rests on sacrificial initiative.

"Husbands, love your wives just as Christ loved the church and gave himself up for her." —Ephesians 5:25

For centuries, men have loved to teach and preach about submission; because in our sinful fallen nature, it sounds great. But we have really misjudged the depth of God's call and command to love our wives as Christ loves the church. Women who have done the pushback towards this verse, because they see it as oppressive, have completely missed this critical link in the spiritual chain.

Jesus does not lead the church in oppression. He pays attention to his bride and feeds his bride. He identifies her needs without her even having to articulate them. He is the groom caring and seeking out ways to satisfy his bride's needs. That means that Jesus is so attuned to you and to me that we didn't even have to discover or realize that we had a sin problem before he provided the solution.

Jesus looked at us and said, "There is a problem here. This relationship for which I've created them has been ruptured by their sin." And in order to solve the problem, he offered himself up. Yes, Jesus leads us. But the vehicle for his leadership is service. When that's happening between a man and a woman, submitting to your husband means that you're submitting to your own best interests.

But it doesn't come naturally or easily. You won't drift

into submission. It requires a conscious decision, an intentionality to make it a reality. And there are some very concrete steps to take toward honoring God in marriage.

Expect sacrificial initiative

First of all, expect sacrificial initiative. Just expect it. You will find that most people play to the level of their expectations. Many times, when you love someone, one of the greatest acts of love is to expect something great from him. Say, "You know what, because I believe in you, I'm not going to let you just skate. I expect you to do what God's called you to do, because I know you're capable of it. I love you."

Look at what Jesus did. He loved the church and gave himself up for her:

> ...*to make her holy, cleansing her by the washing with water through the word. To present her to himself as a radiant church without stain or wrinkle or any other blemish but holy and blameless. In this same way, husbands ought to love their wives as their own bodies. He who loves his wife loves himself. After all, no one ever hated his own body. But he feeds for it and cares for it just as Christ does the church.* —EPHESIANS 5:26-29

A man who doesn't love his wife doesn't love himself. He's got to find out who he is and whose he is in order to love his wife. Again, marriage is no place for Florence Nightingale. If you are dating or single, make sure he's a Christ-chasing servant who is primarily interested in helping you become the woman God created you to be.

If you are already married, lovingly and tenderly expect sacrificial initiative. Make sure that your desire is to help him be the man God created him to be and not just the man you imagine he could be. If your expectations are God's and he's not meeting them, you have a secret weapon to extract them from him.

Extract sacrificial initiative

If extracting sacrificial initiative from your man sounds manipulative, think again. God has very lovingly and intentionally given you a prescription for extracting this from your husband:

> *Wives, in the same way be submissive to your husbands so that, if any of them do not believe the word, they may be won over without words by the behavior of their wives, when they see the purity and reverence of your lives.* —1 Peter 3:1-2

There he goes again with the *submission* thing. It's almost like God is consistent, isn't it? But look at the way he encourages wives to wield submission. It's a tool for relational leverage. Even in the life of a husband who is not a Christ-follower, your submission is an opportunity to SHOW him the love of God, that he "may be won over" —say those next two words out loud—"without words" by your behavior.

When he sees the purity and the reverence of your life, that you are not there to preach at him, you win him over by extracting sacrificial initiative by fanning it into flame when you see it. When you see even a faint, glowing ember back there in the fire somewhere, break out your blacksmith bellows and start fanning that ember into a flame.

If he does something as menial as taking out the trash, show genuine appreciation: "You are so wonderful. Thank for you doing that. I know it may not make sense to you, but that tells me you love me, and I appreciate it so much." We're not just being funny here. A man's primary need in this world is respect. Even before sex, respect is his primary need. If you will fan that fire of respect in him, he will be respectable. When a man feels respected, he feels safe enough to come out of his shell. When he feels even remotely ridiculed or unappreciated, he withdraws.

But even if he is less than respectable, God hasn't called you to submit to your husband for your husband's sake. You submit to him out of reverence for Christ. In that he sees the beauty of God. You become a woman who's not striving or nagging trying to get him to come along. Extract it. Fan it into flame wherever you see it.

Respect sacrificial initiative

Last, respect sacrificial initiative. Respect it.

> *However, each one of you must love his wife as he loves himself and the wife must respect her husband.*
> —EPHESIANS 5:33

It is what it is. When you respect your husband, you respect the authority of God. And the authority of God is what God uses to accomplish his purposes in this world. It is the power of God that he's calling all of us to respect.

Submission is much bigger than just marriage. Submission is the ultimate question between God and a person. People love to talk about grace, forgiveness, love, blessing, hope and joy. And those things are all there. But they're only found in true submission, male or female. Husband or wife. Married, single, or undecided.

Submit to him your life, and in that, receive his life. That is what Christ has done for you on the cross.

You see, Jesus not only calls us to this, he models this. On the night that he was betrayed, the Bible says that Jesus was praying in such anguish knowing what was to come that drops of blood formed on his forehead. And he said, "God, if there's any way for me to avoid the cross and the physical anguish, the spiritual death and separation from you, please let this cup of suffering to pass from me." That prayer we understand. We've all prayed prayers like that before.

But the prayer that followed it is the one that sometimes sticks in our throat, in our heart, because it is so difficult to pray with sincerity:

> *"But not my will, but your will be done."*
> —LUKE 22:42

That's what Jesus did. He submitted himself completely to and through the point of death for you and for me. For someone who loves you that deeply, that unconditionally, that perfectly, submitting to him is submitting to your own best interest.

Chapter 8

THE BEAUTY OF CONTENTMENT

My daughter Emily was five years old on her first trip to Disney World. This was a milestone moment, not only for her, but also for Julie and me since Julie's parents were taking her. It was the first time that she was going to be away from us for an extended period of time.

In preparation for the trip, Julie got her geared up with the necessary provisions: new Keds® for the hours of walking, a little hat and sunglasses to prevent sunburn, and any other fun-gear that this big adventure might require. At the last minute, almost as an afterthought, Julie included a pair of white dress sandals just in case they went out to eat at a restaurant other than one of the park's myriad of dining options.

Since this was Emily's first time away from home, we made sure that we received regular updates by phone about how they were doing, what they were seeing, where they were going. For four full days and three nights, all they did was whatever Emily wanted to do. Homesickness was never even an option for Emily; we missed her much more than she missed us.

When she got home, Julie and I drove to the airport, anxious to hear about her exciting trip and learn about her impressions of the Magic Kingdom. When she saw us standing at the edge of the jet way, she came running toward us, shrieking and giggling to be home. As she jumped into our arms, Julie asked her, "Emily how was Disney World?"

All of a sudden, the shrieking stopped. The giggling died down. The excitement vanished. Emily looked my wife dead in the eye and very somberly said, "Mommy, I didn't get to wear my white sandals, not even once."

Enough—someday

There is something in all of us that always wants just a little bit more, no matter what we have. A little more excitement. A little more stuff. Just more. Whether it's time, peace, height, fitness. Whatever. We just want more. And we convince ourselves that just a little bit more will be enough—someday.

This drive for *enough—someday* really comes from a couple of different places. One of them is God. The desire to advance, to move forward, is something that God has stamped into our souls. Remember, we are created in his image. And God isn't static. He's dynamic, always progressing, always advancing. And so some of our drive for more comes from his character and personality.

However, like any other God-given drive, there's a counterfeit that we fall victim to. Some of this drive, the harmful part, comes from our very humanity. Go back to the Garden of Eden. Adam and Eve had everything: intimacy with God, a thriving marriage, fulfilling and challenging work, and adequate time for rest and refueling.

And yet, they wanted more.

They abandoned their God-given place in the world, their God-given provisions, and their God-given peace—all in their self-centered drive for more.

And we have inherited this drive for more, this longing for *enough—someday* mentality. It's a part of who we are as human beings. It may manifest itself materially: *Someday, if I had more stuff (a bigger house, a cooler car, sweeter clothes…), then I would be OK.*

It might also appear in our relational longings: *Someday, if my dad/husband/kids/friends would just _____, then I would be the greatest, most well-adjusted daughter/wife/ mother/friend you've ever seen.*

This out-of-control drive can also reveal itself in our

excuses: *Someday, if I had more money (or a better childhood, or a better career, or fewer obligations…), then you would see someone really generous (or joyful, or fulfilled, or peaceful, or thoughtful…).*

But here's the reality: If my responsibility, my success, my generosity, my joy, compassion, and comfort are dependent on how much or how much *more* I have, then that someday is never going to arrive. E*nough—someday* is a mirage. The second that we see that something looming on the horizon and begin to take a step towards it, it backs up. It's chasing infinity.

Enough—today

Into the gaping black hole of *enough—someday*, Jesus provides an alternative. Specifically, he offers himself as the sole Provider of Enough. Today.

He holds the secret to *enough—today*, to authentic, soul-filling, life-giving beauty. And that secret is contentment.

We'll give that statement some texture in a moment, but first, think about this question: what's more beautiful than true contentment? When you see a woman who is neither striving to attain something nor hiding the beauty in her life, you see a woman that possesses a kind of peace and contentment that is a work of beauty to behold.

Let's return to Eden. When Eve was simply and completely *there* for her husband, neither striving after what God had forbidden nor hiding behind fig leaves or animal skins, she was full of beauty. She was content within her relationship with God. And because of that relationship, she was content with herself. And, in turn, because of her personal contentment, she was content with her husband.

She wasn't dependent upon Adam for her peace of mind; rather, she looked to him to supplement and complement all that she was getting out of her relationship with God. And out of that contentment, her husband found her truly beautiful. He valued and treasured her. And their relationship embodied what God had in mind when he created them.

Adam and Eve lived out for us a full-color, high-definition picture of an eternal law:

Contentment is a choice.

Our contentment has nothing to do with what we have or don't have. Our contentment is rooted—or not—in the depth of our relationship with God.

It is imperative to understand that this choice rests solely within your control. No other person will ever make you content. No set of circumstances will ever make you content. You have to choose contentment.

If you struggle with contentment, there are three simple, yet profound questions that you can ask yourself to make sure you're on the right track. These questions are born out of a particularly poignant letter found in the New Testament; specifically, Paul's letter to the Philippians.

In Philippians 4, Paul is writing to the church in Philippi to encourage them and teach them how to access the peace of God. Repeatedly, throughout the letter, he tells them to *choose* to dwell on things of beauty, excellence, and truth in order to live in the peace of God that surpasses all understanding, comprehension, or explanation.

So the first question that we ask ourselves:

Am I grateful or grasping?

If you were to characterize your approach to finances, or relationships, or circumstances, are you more grateful for what you have now, or are you always grasping for what you don't have?

Read and reflect on Paul's encouragement to the church at Philippi:

> *Rejoice in the Lord always. I will say it again: Rejoice! Let your gentleness be evident to all. The Lord is near. Do not be anxious about anything, but in everything, by prayer and petition, with thanksgiving, present your*

requests to God. And the peace of God, which tran-
scends all understanding, will guard your hearts and
your minds in Christ Jesus.   —PHILIPPIANS 4:4-7

Rejoice. That simply means to celebrate! And Paul feels so deeply and passionately about this that he says it twice.

In *everything* give thanks. In other words, be grateful for every circumstance, every possession, every relationship, *every*thing. Say regularly, "God, thank you for what you're showing me about your strength in my weakness. Thank you for what you're giving me. Thank you for my spouse. Thank you."

It's easy to be thankful when life is good, when things are going your way. It's hard, though, to be thankful when things aren't going so well. But Paul is specifically telling us here that we need to be grateful in every situation because that is a key to contentment.

The second contentment question is this:

Am I peaceful or fearful?

If fear is a major factor in your life, there's probably a disconnect somewhere in your gratitude chain. If we are stressed out and worried all the time, then we haven't really stepped back and said, "God, thank you. Every morning your mercy continues to astound me. Your faithfulness is constant."

Real contentment transcends socio-economic status, marital status, and anything-else status. Look again at Philippians 4.

I am not saying this because I am in need, for I have learned to be content whatever the circumstances. I know what it is to be in need, and I know what it is to have plenty. I have learned the secret of being content in any and every situation, whether well fed or hungry, whether living in plenty or in want. —Philippians 4:11-12

Again, Paul is writing this letter to the church at Philippi to encourage them. He's also writing to thank them for the financial gift they had sent him to further his ministry. It's a thank-you note. He's saying, "You people have knocked it out of the ballpark. The joy that you have shown in your generosity and providing for my needs and providing for ministry is amazing. Thank you, thank you, thank you."

You might read this and think, "No wonder Paul is content. He just received money from those generous Philippians! His circumstances are looking pretty good."

While that's true, there's one little detail to remember about Paul's circumstances: he's writing this letter from a Roman prison. And it's from this prison cell that Paul is writing unapologetically about the secret of contentment in "any and every situation."

Many of us go through life thinking we're facing difficult situations. We sit in traffic and complain. We come home and whine about the dirty dishes that have piled up. We wonder why we have so many bills to pay. But remember, Paul was chained to a Roman guard! And *he's* the one showing us how to be content.

The third contentment question leads us ultimately into the *enough—today* destination:

Am I pro-active or re-active?

Paul said in verse 12 that he has learned the secret of contentment. Then in verse 13 he shares the secret:

> *I can do everything through him who gives me strength.*
> —Philippians 4:13

Look at the first three words: *I can do.* In Christ, you can *do.* You can act. You can move. You can help, serve, give, plan, work, teach, equip, encourage, correct. You can. But it takes action on your part.

In God's economy, contentment never devolves into complacency or passivity. It is always active, dynamic, proactive. Remember, it's God's design in our lives to reflect his nature. And God is anything but passive!

Godly contentment always claims victory rather than

victimizing. The experience of soul-deep contentment depends on accepting your role, your God-given responsibility to take care of the time, talent, and treasure that he has chosen to give you. To be fully content, be pro-active. *I can do everything.* Everything.

But the ability to do *everything* is conditional. Paul says, "I can do everything *through Him who gives me strength.*" You can do everything, but only through him.

In John 15, Jesus said,

Remain in me, and I will remain in you. No branch can bear fruit by itself; it must remain in the vine. Neither can you bear fruit unless you remain in me. "I am the vine; you are the branches. If a man remains in me and I in him, he will bear much fruit; apart from me you can do nothing." —JOHN 15:4-5

In him, everything. Apart from him, nothing.

Have you personally, definitively, and completely given yourself to Christ? He has already declared you beautiful. Through his cross, you are restored to a beauty that transcends mere physical appearance. Your value as a woman, as a person, as a child of God is absolutely and completely undeniable.

He has proclaimed that through his cross you never have

to hide your beauty or strive for something you don't have. In him, because of his cross, you can find rest. In him, you can reveal his glory through your thoughts, motives, words and actions.

God has invited you into that peace, that contentment, that true beauty that wells up in your soul and radiates out through your life, your presence. And that beauty blesses everyone you meet, every member of your extended family, every person in your home. And it is available in a personal relationship with Jesus.

Stepping into a personal relationship with Christ is remarkably straightforward. It's not easy or cheap, but it is beautiful in its simplicity. Like every other relationship, it requires communication. If you have never stepped over the line of faith, ask him into your life right now. In your own words, from your heart to his, pray a prayer of commitment like this one:

Dear Jesus, my heart's desire is to be as you created me to be—beautiful, not only in appearance, but also in my heart. Right now, I choose to believe that on the cross, you carried my sin. I choose to believe that you died a death that was rightfully mine. I admit to you and to myself that I have sinned. I confess it to you and all its ugliness.

But I choose to believe that you rose from the dead

for me. And that in your resurrection is my new life. Jesus, I accept you. And in exchange for your life, I give you mine. Everything I am, everything I will ever be is yours. Jesus, thank you. Thank you for giving me your beauty. I pray this in your name, Amen.

It is this relationship that brings us full circle to the original intent of the beauty of Eden. Everything that we ever need is found in fellowship with God. It is that connection that reveals to us true beauty—in spirit and in form. It is that relationship that repairs the ugliness of our sin and redeems us through grace and mercy. It is through Jesus that God has restored and reconciled himself to us—by the truth and grace of God himself.

If you are already a Christ-follower, then you know the beauty of Jesus, of the one who came as the only child of the Father, full of grace and truth. You know that through his cross he has redeemed you from your sin and made all things new.

But do you know—do you *really* know—that contentment, that peace that surpasses all understanding? Are you doing *all things* through him who gives you strength? Whenever you doubt your beauty, hide your beauty, or strive too hard after a cosmetic façade, know that your doubt and insecurity is not from God, but from Satan—your enemy who has done nothing but attempt to destroy your life from the beginning.

Remember, Jesus is your advocate, forgiver, truth-teller, giver, and creator from *before* the beginning and throughout all eternity. And his promises are faithful, constant, and truly beauty full.

Mac and I have spent years together in ministry and in life. And some of our earliest and strongest connections were made during beach retreats for high school and middle school students.

And as those trips have changed and evolved through the years, they are still marked by some uncanny constants: sunburned boys because they refused to use sunscreen; girls who spend hours getting ready for dinner and evening services so they look casual and carefree; and the undeniable hand of God as he touches, calls, convicts, and leads young people toward the life he designed them to live.

Another constant is a song that my dad has insisted on including in the corporate worship of these trips every year. And even as styles have changed and students have become more sophisticated and exposed to life, there is a song written in 1973 that resonates with the beauty Jesus shares with every one who walks with him:

Something beautiful, something good
All my confusion, he understood
All I had to offer him
Was brokenness and strife
But he made something beautiful of my life.

Take hold of his beauty, because his beauty is your beauty.

Eternally. Irrevocably. Today.